Poems of Love

A Treasury of Verse

Illustrated by Zita Asbaghi

Running Press
Philadelphia ◊ London

Canadian representatives: General Publishing Co., Ltd., 30
Lesmill Road, Don Mills, Ontario M3B 2T6.
Library of Congress Cataloging-in-Publication Number
93-083463

ISBN 1-56138-309-0

This book may be ordered by mail from the publisher.
Please include $1.00 for postage and handling.
But try your bookstore first!

Running Press Book Publishers
125 South Twenty-second Street
Philadelphia, Pennsylvania 19103

Introduction

The shy gift of friendship, first sparks, fiery passion, unrequited ardor: love reveals itself in many ways. Touching every aspect of our lives, love has no boundaries of time or place.

Poets have always sought to express this most elusive and contradictory of emotions. Gathered here are poets' words of lovers and their beloved, from Shakespeare to D. H. Lawrence, from Emily Dickinson to e.e. cummings.

Essence

OF LOVE

Love is anterior to life,
     Posterior to death,
Initial of creation, and
     The exponent of breath.

Emily Dickinson (1830–1886)
American poet

. . .Give all to love;
Obey thy heart;
Friends, kindred, days,
Estate, good fame,
Plans, credit, and the Muse—
Nothing refuse.

'Tis a brave master;
Let it have scope:
Follow it utterly,
Hope beyond hope:

High and more high

It dives into noon,

With wing unspent,

Untold intent;

But it is a god,

Knows its own path,

And the outlets of the sky....

Ralph Waldo Emerson (1803–1882)
American writer

...the Love which us **doth** bind,

But Fate so enviously d **ebars**,

Is the Conjunction of t **he** Mind,

And opposition of the **Stars**.

From "The Definition of Love"
Andrew Marvell (1621–1678)
English poet

What thing is love? for, well I
    wot, love is a thing.

It is a prick, it is a sting,

It is a pretty pretty thing;

It is a fire, it is a coal,

Whose flame creeps in at
    every hole;

And as my wit doth best devise,

Love's dwelling is in ladies' eyes:

From whence do glance love's
    piercing darts

That make such holes
    into our hearts;

And all the world herein accord

Love is a great and mighty lord,

And when he list to mount
    so high,

With Venus he in heaven doth lie,

And evermore hath been a god

Since Mars and she played even
    and odd.

"What Thing Is Love?"
George Peele (1558–1597)
English poet

. . .Oh, let the solid ground
   Not fail beneath my feet
Before my life has found
   What some have found
     so sweet!

Then let come what may,
What matter if I go mad,
I shall have had my day.

Alfred, Lord Tennyson (1809—1892)
English poet

True love is but a humble
low-born thing,

And hath its food served up in
earthen ware;

It is a thing to walk with,
hand in hand,

Through the every-dayness of
this work-day world.

"True Love"
James Russell Lowell (1819–1892)
American writer

We're all waiting for t**h**e supreme

love poem to **w**r**i**te itself

all around us witho**u**t

break, n**o**

moment l**e**ft

untou**c**hed by

love's

signatures, n**o**

glance out window **o**r **o**nto

distant mounta**i**n side

sheen-filled with new **w**ildflowers

. . .without

love's

spectacular script writin**g**

   itself first

     in quick electri**c** **s**q**uiggles**

    over

      everything **we** see.

From "Handwriting"
Abd al-Hayy Moore, b. 1940
American poet

...But love is a durable fire

In the mind ever burning;

Never sick, never old, never dead

From itself never turning.

Sir Walter Raleigh (1552?–1598)
English writer

Love blows as the **wind** blows.

Blows!...in the quiet **c**lose

As in the roaring **mart**,

By ways no mortal **knows**

Love blows into the **hea**rt.

The stars some cad**enc**e use.

Forthright the river **flo**ws,

In order fall the dew**s**,

Love blows as the **wind** blows;

Blows! . . . and what
      reckoning shows

The courses of his chart?

A spirit that comes and goes,

Love blows into the heart.

From "To K. De M."
William Ernest Henley (1849–1903)
English poet

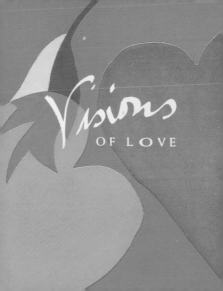

Visions

OF LOVE

. . . I whispered, 'I am too young,

And then, 'I am old enough';

Wherefore I threw a penny

To find out if I might love.

'Go and love, go and love,
          young man,

If the lady be young and fair.'

Ah, penny, brown penny,
          brown penny,

I am looped in the loops of her hair.

From "Brown Penny"
William Butler Yeats (1865–1939)
Irish poet

She walks in beauty, like the night

Of cloudless climes and
starry skies;

And all that's best of dark
and bright

Meet in her aspect and her eyes:

Thus mellow'd to that tender light

Which heaven to gaudy day
denies . . . .

From "She Walks In Beauty"
George Gordon, Lord Byron (1788 – 1824)
English poet

My mistress' eyes are **n**othing like
the sun;

Coral is far more red **th**an her
lips' red:

If snow be white, why **t**hen her
breasts are dun;

If hairs be wires, bla**ck** wires grow
on her head.

I have seen roses dam**a**sked,
red and white,

But no such roses se**e** I in
her cheeks

And in some perfum**es** is there
more delight

Than in the breath that from my
mistress reeks.

I love to hear her speak; yet
well I know

That music hath a far more
pleasing sound:

I grant I never saw a goddess go,

My mistress, when she walks,
treads on the ground:

And yet, by heaven, I think my
love as rare

As any she belied with
false compare.

"Sonnet CXXX"
William Shakespeare (1564–1616)
English writer

When she rises in the morning

I linger to watch her;

She spreads the bath-cloth
      underneath the window

And the sunbeams catch her

Glistening white on the shoulders,

While down her sides the mellow

Golden shadow glows as

She stoops to the sponge, and her
      swung breasts

Sway like full-blown yellow

Gloire de Dijon roses.

She drips herself with water, and
    her shoulders

Glisten as silver, they crumple up

Like wet and falling roses, and
    I listen

For the sluicing of their
    rain-dishevelled petals.

In the window full of sunlight

Concentrates her golden shadow

Fold on fold, until it glows as

Mellow as the glory roses.

"Gloire De Dijon"
D. H. Lawrence (1855–1930)
English writer

She wore a new "terra-cotta"
dress,

And we stayed, because of the
pelting storm,

Within the hansom's dry recess,

Though the horse had stopped;
yea, motionless

We sat on, snug and warm.

Then the downpour ceased, to my
sharp sad pain

And the glass that had screened
our forms before

Flew up, and out she sprang to
the door:

I should have kissed her if the rain

Had lasted a minute more.

"A Thunderstorm in Town"
Thomas Hardy (1840–1928)
English writer

Kiss me as if you made believe
You were not sure, this eve,
How my face, your flower,
        had pursed
Its petals up; so, here and there
You brush it, till I grow aware
Who wants me, and wide ope
        I burst.

From "In a Gondola"
Robert Browning (1812–1889)
English poet

'I saw you take his kiss!' ''Tis true.'

'O, modesty!' ''Twas
strictly kept:

He thought me asleep; at least
I knew

He thought I thought he
thought I slept.'

"The Kiss"
Coventry Patmore (1823–1896)
English poet

An orange on the table

Your dress on the rug

    And you in my bed

Sweet present of the present

    Cool of night

Warmth of my life.

"Alicante"
Jacques Prevert (1900–1977)
French poet

Thus do I fall to rise thus,

Thus do I dye to live thus,

Changed to a change, I
change not.

Thus may I not be from you:

Thus be my senses on you:

Thus what I thinke is of you:

Thus what I seeke is in you:

All what I am, it is you.

Sir Philip Sidney (1554–1586)
English poet

The simple lack
Of her is more to me
Than others' presence
Whether life splendid be
Or utter black.

I have not seen,
I have no news of her;
I can tell only
She is not here, but there
She might have been.

From "The Unknown"
Edward Thomas (1887–1917)
English poet

Lying asleep between the strokes
   of night
    I saw my love lean over my
     sad bed,

    Pale as the duskiest lily's leaf
     or head,

Smooth-skinned and dark, with
    bare throat made to bite,

Too wan for blushing and too
    warm for white,

    But perfect-coloured without
    white or red.

And her lips opened
    amorously, and said—

I wist not what, saving one
    word—Delight.

And all her face was honey
    to my mouth,

    And all her body pasture to
        mine eyes;

        The long lithe arms and
            hotter hands
            than fire

The quivering flanks, hair
smelling of the south,

The bright light feet, the
splendid supple thighs

And glittering eyelids of
my soul's desire.

"Love and Sleep"
Algernon Charles Swinburne (1837–1909)
English poet

. . . Love!—maker of my lady,

in that always beyond this

poem or any poem she

of whose body words are afraid

perfectly beautiful is,

forgive these words which i
    have made.

e. e. cummings (1894–1962)
American poet

Seasons

OF LOVE

The Spring comes in with all her
hues and smells

In freshness breathing over hills
and dells;

O'er woods where May her
gorgeous drapery flings,

And meads washed fragrant by
their laughing springs.

Fresh are new opened flowers,
untouched and free

From the bold rifling of an
amorous bee.

The happy time of singing birds
　　is come,

And Love's lone pilgrimage now
　　finds a home;

Among the mossy oaks now coos
　　the dove,

And the hoarse crow finds softer
　　notes for love.

The foxes play around their dens,
　　and bark

In joy's excess, 'mid woodland
　　shadows dark.

The flowers join lips below; the
leaves above;

And every sound that meets the
ear is Love.

"A Spring Morning"
John Clare (1793–1864)
English poet

. . .Under the summer roses,

When the fragrant crimson

Lurks in the dusk

Of the wild red leaves,

Love, with little hands,

Comes and touches you

With a thousand memories,

And asks you

Beautiful, unanswerable
        questions.

Carl Sandburg (1878–1967)
American poet

You say you have been **d r**enched
        waiting for me
on the foothill-trailing **m o**untain.
O that I could be

that trickling rain!

"*Poem Presented To Lady Ishikawa
        In Response*"
Prince Otsu
3rd-century Chinese poet

...even as water cou**l****d** you touch
and behold

my heart, as through our hands
it flowed...

Sor Juana Ines de la Cruz (1652–1695)
Mexican poet

Hot sun, cool fire, tempered with
  sweet air,

Black shade, fair nurse, shadow
  my white hair,

Shine, sun, burn, fire, breathe,
  air, and ease me,

Black shade, fair nurse, shroud
  me and please me;

Shadow, my sweet nurse, keep me
  from burning,

Make not glad cause, cause
  of morning.

Love made me such that I live
in fire

like a new salamander on earth

or like that other rare creature,
the Phoenix,

who expires and rises at
the same time.

Gaspara Stampa (c. 1520–1554)
Italian poet

my arms grow beautiful

in the coupling

and grow lean

as they come away.

What shall I make of this?

"What She Said to Her Girl-Friend"
Anonymous 3rd-century Indian poet

On beaches washed by seas
Older than the earth
in the groves filled with
        bird-cries,
on the banks shaded and
clustered with flowers,
        when we made love
my eyes saw him
and my ears heard him;

. . . I asked him with my eyes to
ask again yes and then he asked
me would I yes to say yes my
mountain flower and first I put
my arms around him yes and drew
him down to me so he could feel
my breasts all perfume yes and
his heart was going like mad and
yes I said yes I will Yes.

From "Ulysses"
James Joyce (1882–1941)
Irish writer

Let not my beauty's fire

Inflame unstaid desire,

Nor pierce any bright eye

That wandereth lightly.

"Bethsabe's Song" from
  "David and Bethsabe"
George Peele (1558–1597)
English poet

. . . Down there we satt upon
the Moss,

And did begin to play

A Thousand Amorous Tricks,
to pass

The heat of all the day.

A many Kisses he did give:

And I return'd the same

Which made me willing to receive

That which I dare not name.

From "The Willing Mistriss"
Aphra Behn (1640–1689)
English poet

Recklessly

I cast myself away;

Perhaps

A heart in love

Becomes a deep ravine?

Izumi Shikibu
10th-century Japanese poet

. . . High heaven causes a girl's
lovelonging.

It is like being too far from
the light,

Far from the hearth of familiar
arms.

It is this being so tangled
in you.

From "Love of You is Mixed Deep
in My Vitals"
Anonymous Egyptian poet

Song

OF LOVE

I'll love you dear, I'll love you

    Till China and Africa meet

And the river jumps over
      the mountain

    And the salmon sings in
      the street.

I'll love you till the ocean

    Is folded and hung up to dry

And the seven stars go squawking

    Like geese about in the sky.

W. H. Auden (1907–1973)
English-born American poet

I looked and saw your eyes
  In the shadow of your hair,
As a traveler sees the stream
  In the shadow of the wood;
And I said, "My faint heart sighs,
  Ah me! to linger there,
To drink deep and to dream
  In that sweet solitude."

I looked and saw your heart
  In the shadow of your eyes,

As a seeker sees the gold
    In the shadow of the stream;
And I said, "Ah me! what art
    Should win the immortal
      prize,
Whose want must make life cold
    And heaven a hollow dream?"

I looked and saw your love
    In the shadow of your heart,
As a diver sees the pearl
    In the shadow of the sea;

And I murmured, not above

   My breath, but all apart—

"Ah! you can love, true girl,

   And is your love for me?"

"Three Shadows"
Dante Gabriel Rossetti (1828–1882)
English poet

I do not love thee!—no! I do
    not love thee!

And yet when thou art absent
    I am sad;

    And envy even the bright blue
        sky above thee,

Whose quiet stars may see thee
        and be glad.

    I do not love thee!—yet, I
        know not why,

Whate'er thou dost seems still
        well done, to me:

And often in my solitude I sigh
That those I do love are not more
like thee!

I do not love thee!—yet, when
thou art gone,
I hate the sound (though those
who speak be dear)
Which breaks the lingering
echo of the tone
Thy voice of music leaves
upon my ear.

I do not love thee!—yet, thy
speaking eyes,

With their deep, bright, and most
expressive blue,

Between me and the midnight
heaven arise,

Oftener than any eyes I
ever knew.

I know I do not love thee!
yet, alas!

Others will scarcely trust my
   candid heart;

   And oft I catch them smiling as
      they pass,

Because they see me gazing
      where thou art.

"I do not love thee"
Caroline Elizabeth Sarah Norton
(1808–1877)
English writer

. . .Come live with me and
be my Love,

And we will all the pleasures
prove

That hills and valleys, dales
and fields,

Or woods or steepy mountain
yields.

And we will sit upon the rocks,

And see the shepherds feed
their flocks

By shallow rivers, to whose falls

Melodious birds sing
madrigals....

From "The Passionate Shepherd to His Love"
Christopher Marlowe (1564–1593)
English poet

If ever two were one, then
  surely we.

If man were loved by wife,
  then thee;

If ever wife was happy in a man,

Compare with me, ye women,
  if you can.

I prize thy love more than whole
  mines of gold

Or all the riches that the   East
    doth hold.

My love is such that rive **rs**
    cannot quench,

Nor ought but love from   thee,
    give recompense.

Thy love is such I can
    no way repay,

The heavens reward the   manifold,
    I pray.

Then while we live, in love let's
    so persever

That when we live no more, we
    may live ever.

"To My Dear and Loving Husband"
Anne Bradstreet (1612–1672)
American poet

One word is too of**t** **e**n profaned

   For me to profan **e** it;

One feeling too fals **e**ly disdain'd

   For thee to disda **i** n it;

One hope is too like despair

   For prudence to s **m**other;

And pity from thee **m** **o**re dear

   Than that from an **o**ther.

I can give not what men call love

    But wilt thou accept not

The worship the heart lifts above

    And the heavens reject not,

The desire of the moth for

    the star,

    Of the night for the morow,

The devotion to something afar

    From the sphere of our

    sorrow?

"To ———"
Percy Bysshe Shelley (1792–1822)
English poet

Who can wonder then, if **thou**

Hearest breathe my tend**er** vow;

If thy lips, so pure, so br**i**ght,

Are dim with kisses, day
and night?

W. S. Landor (1775–1864)
English writer

Oh, think not I am faithful
to a vow!

Faithless am I save to love's
self alone.

Were you not lovely I would leave
you now:

After the feet of beauty
fly my own.

Were you not still my hunger's
rarest food,

And water ever to my wildest
thirst,

I would desert you—think not
   but I would!—
And seek another as I sought
   you first.
But you are mobile as
   the veering air,
And all your charms more
   changeful than the tide,
Wherefore to be inconstant
   is no care:
I have but to continue at
   your side.

So wanton, light an d false, my
love, are you,

I am most faithless w hen I most
am true.

Edna St. Vincent Millay (1892~1950)
American poet

. . . I love not for those eyes,
     nor haire,

Nor cheekes, nor lips, nor teeth
     so rare;

Nor for thy speech, thy necke,
     nor breast,

Nor for thy belly, nor the rest:

Nor for thy hand, nor foote
     so small,

But wouldst thou know (deere
     sweet) for all.

From "The Complement"
Thomas Carew (1595–1639)
English poet

With you here at Mertu
Is like being at Heliopolis already.

We return to the tree-filled garden,
My arms full of flowers.

Looking at my reflection in
       the still pool—
My arms full of flowers—

I see you creeping on tip-toe
To kiss me from behind,
My hair heavy with perfume.

With your arms around me
I feel as if I belong to
    the Pharaoh.

Anonymous Egyptian poet (1567–1085 B.C.)

. . . If love were what the rose is,

    And I were like the leaf,

Our lives would grow together

In sad or singing weather,

Blown fields or flowerful closes,

    Green pleasure or grey grief;

If love were what the rose is,

    And I were like the leaf. . . .

From "A Match"
Algernon Charles Swinburne (1837–1909)
English poet

Alter? When the hills **do**.

Falter? When the sun

Question if his glory

Be the perfect one.

Emily Dickinson (1830–1886)
American poet

How do I love thee? Let me count
the ways.

I love thee to the depth and
breadth and height

My soul can reach, when feeling
out of sight

For the ends of Being and
ideal Grace.

I love thee to the level
of every day's

Most quiet need, by sun and
candlelight.

I love thee freely, as me **n** strive
    for Right;

I love thee purely, as th **ey** turn
    from Praise.

I love thee with the pas **sion**
    put to use

In my old griefs, and wi **t** h my
    childhood's faith **.**

I love thee with a love I **seemed**
    to lose

With my lost saints,—I **love** thee
    with the breath,

Smiles, tears, of all **my** life!—
and, if God cho**o**se,

I shall love thee bett**e r** after death.

"Sonnet XLIII"
*Elizabeth Barrett Browning (**1 8** 06–1861)*
English poet

This book has been bound using handcraft methods,
and Smyth-sewn to ensure durability.

The dust jacket was designed by Toby Schmidt.
The cover and interior illustrations were by Zita Asbaghi.
The interior was designed by Stephanie Longo.

The text was compiled by David Borgenicht and
edited by Melissa Stein.

The text was set in Weiss by Deborah Lugar.

Text Acknowledgments

Pp. 18–19: Copyright © 1993 by Abd al-Hayy Moore, reprinted by permission of
the author; pp. 30–31: "Gloire de Dijon," from *The Complete Poems of D. H.
Lawrence* by D. H. Lawrence, copyright © 1964, 1971 by Angelo Ravagli and
M. Weekley, Executors of the Estate of Frieda Lawrence Ravagli, reprinted by
permission of Viking Penguin, a division of Penguin Books USA Inc.; p. 36: Copyright
© 1959 by Lawrence Ferlinghetti, reprinted by permission of City Lights Books;
p. 53: Excerpt from *Ulysses: The Corrected Text* by James Joyce, reading text
copyright © 1984 by The Trustees of the Estate of James Joyce, reprinted by
permission of Random House, Inc. and Jonathan Cape; p. 61: Poem from *The Izumi
Shikibu Diary*, translated by Edwin A. Cranston, copyright © 1969 Harvard-Yenching
Institute, reprinted by permission of Harvard University press; p. 63: Excerpt from
"Love of You is Mixed Deep in My Vitals" from *Love Songs of the New Kingdom*,
translated and illustrated by John L. Foster, published by the University of Texas
Press in 1992, reprinted by permission of the publisher; p. 66: From *W. H. Auden:
Collected Poems* by W. H. Auden, edited by Edward Mendelson, copyright © 1944
renewed 1968 by W. H. Auden, reprinted by permission of Random House, Inc.
and Faber and Faber Ltd.; pp. 84–86: "Oh, think not that I am faithful to a vow"
by Edna St. Vincent Millay, from *Collected Poems*, published by HarperCollins,
copyright © 1922, 1950 by Edna St. Vincent Millay. Copyright © 1950 by Norma
Elizabeth Barnett, literary executor; pp. 88–89: From Ezra Pound: *Love Poems of
Ancient Egypt*, copyright © 1962 by Noel Stock, reprinted by permission of New
Directions Publishing Corporation.